A Human Being Made This

A HUMAN BEING ILLUSTRATED THIS STORY

Kathleen Connors

CREATED BY Humans

Published in 2026 by The Rosen Publishing Group, Inc.
2544 Clinton Street, Buffalo, NY 14224

First Edition

Editor: Kristen Nelson
Designer: Michael Flynn

Photo Credits: Cover, p. 11 Tanya_Terekhina/Shutterstock.com; (series background) Yuliya Chsherbakova; p. 5 PeopleImages.com - Yuri A/Shutterstock.com; p. 7 (top) Improvisor/Shutterstock.com; p. 7 (bottom) Bartek Winnicki/Shutterstock.com; p. 9 Pressmaster/Shutterstock.com; p. 13 Stefan.Simonovski/Shutterstock.com; p. 15 Ellianne/Shutterstock.com; p. 17 https://commons.wikimedia.org/wiki/File:Todd_Parr_Book.jpg; p. 19 Ermolaeva Olga 84/Shutterstock.com; p. 21 Prostock-studio/Shutterstock.com.

Cataloging-in-Publication Data

Names: Connors, Kathleen.
Title: A human being illustrated this story / Kathleen Connors.
Description: Buffalo, NY : Created by Humans, an imprint of Rosen Publishing, 2026. | Series: A human being made this | Includes glossary and index.
Identifiers: ISBN 9781534552579 (pbk.) | ISBN 9781534552586 (library bound) | ISBN 9781534552593 (ebook)
Subjects: LCSH: Drawing--Technique--Juvenile literature. | Cartooning--Technique--Juvenile literature. | AI art--Juvenile literature.
Classification: LCC NC710.C66 2026 | DDC 741.21--dc23

Manufactured in China

CPSIA Compliance Information: Batch #QWCBH26. For Further Information contact Rosen Publishing at 1-800-237-9932.

CONTENTS

MORE THAN A PICTURE

Illustrations are the pictures—including diagrams and charts—that **support** a piece of writing. You are probably most familiar with illustrations in stories. In picture books, the illustrations are just as important as the text, or words, of the story. They create the look of the world and the **characters** in it.

Today, AI **technology** is so advanced that it can be used to create illustrations. Until now, all illustrations were created by humans! This will affect how books are made for years to come.

GET THE FACTS

AI stands for artificial intelligence.

Do you know if your favorite story or book series was illustrated by a person or by AI?

GenAI

Artificial intelligence includes computer programs that can learn over time. AI can look at a large amount of data very quickly. It can solve problems and find patterns. In addition, it can get better over time.

Generative AI, or GenAI, uses the data it has been given to create something, such as a picture. It must be given a prompt, but it can create a picture very quickly—a lot faster than a person can plan, draw, and color an illustration.

GET THE FACTS

A prompt is the written directions to do something.

Midjourney and DALL-E 3 are two GenAI tools that can be used to make an illustration.

PROBLEMS WITH GenAI

GenAI may be fast, but it's only as good as the prompt it has been given. And, sometimes AI makes pictures in which people have six fingers or three legs! Furthermore, some AI technology has been trained using **copyrighted** content.

The main problem with using GenAI to illustrate something is that the art is missing you! The **perspective** you, the artist, brings to an illustration is what makes it special. GenAI cannot copy the creative spark of a human!

GET THE FACTS

Using copyrighted content without permission—including to train AI—is illegal.

GenAI might make an illustration quickly, but it cannot express feelings through art like a person can.

TYPES OF ILLUSTRATIONS

Look through the books on your bookshelf and you will see many different illustration **styles**. Some are clearly drawn and painted by hand. These may look very true to life. Others may be hand drawn but look like cartoons.

Illustrations can be created on a computer or tablet using **software** like Adobe Illustrator. A person is still using their hands to create digital art. They are still making all the choices about the lines, colors, and composition.

GET THE FACTS

Composition has to do with the way the parts of a picture are put together and arranged.

Digital illustrators are still artists even though they use different tools.

AN ILLUSTRATOR'S JOB

An illustrator's work allows readers to see what's happening in a story, even if the reader can't read yet. Illustrations make a funny scene funnier. Showing what a character's face looks like lets the reader know how they feel even if it's not in the text.

Illustrators may work with an author to create a story together. They may create the art of a story after the writing is finished. Finally, some illustrators both write the words and draw pictures for a story!

GET THE FACTS

Illustrators may also work for magazines, websites, and other companies that need someone to create **visuals**.

An illustrator's work is important to the success of a story.

QUENTIN BLAKE

Born near London, England, in 1932, illustrator Quentin Blake started drawing at a very young age. He studied drawing and started putting out his work in magazines when he was just a teenager! He illustrated his first children's book in 1960.

Blake starts a project by doing a rough drawing. Then, he uses a **light box** to make the drawing again, using the first one as a guide. Later, he uses watercolors to fill in the drawing. He may make two or more **versions** of each illustration.

GET THE FACTS

Blake says he stops and starts a drawing over many times. He wants to make sure he gets every piece of the picture just right.

Blake is widely known for illustrating books by Roald Dahl, including *Matilda, The BFG,* and *Charlie and the Chocolate Factory*.

TODD PARR

Todd Parr is a book illustrator with a style that stands out! He also writes the text that goes into his books.

Parr creates books for kids. His illustrations are simple. They have bright colors and thick, bold, black outlines. In some of his books, it says how he created the art. It says he uses a drawing tablet to start with the thick black lines. Then he puts the color in using a computer program called Adobe Photoshop.

GET THE FACTS

Parr worked as a flight attendant before he created books for a living. His first book came out in 1999: *The Okay Book*.

Parr writes and illustrates books with uplifting messages. They encourage kids to be themselves and not be scared of having feelings.

FIND INSPIRATION

A great place to start looking for illustration **inspiration** is the library. You can ask a librarian to help you find books with famously good illustrations. This way, you can see what kinds of artwork make a story really stand out.

Then, spend time picking up picture books that look cool, pretty, or interesting. Think about what you like about the illustrations. Consider taking some of those books out to show your art teacher. Your teacher can help you understand different styles.

GET THE FACTS

Many communities have art classes for kids. Talk to your family or art teacher about finding one that works for you.

A library is a great place to look at books that have been illustrated.

START DRAWING!

Are you ready to start illustrating? Get your paper and pencils or digital drawing tools ready and try one of these ideas:

- Illustrate a scene from your favorite non-illustrated book.
- Choose your favorite illustrator and create your own scene **imitating** their style.
- Have a friend write a short story. Draw the pictures to go along with it.
- Think of a character from a video game you like. Imagine them in a normal situation, such as at school. Illustrate it!

TRY THIS!

Write a prompt for one of the ideas above and enter it into a GenAI program. What does it create? Compare the GenAI art to your own. What do you like about each of them? What makes yours special?

Your perspective, feelings, and drawing style are what make your illustrations different from anyone else's—including anything made by GenAI.

GLOSSARY

character: Someone who appears in a book or movie.

copyrighted: Having to do with copyright, which is the legal right to be the only one to reproduce, publish, and sell a book, recording, or something else for a time period.

imitate: Copy.

inspiration: An event, piece of art, or action that causes someone to want to do something.

light box: A tool that puts out strong, even light.

perspective: Point of view.

software: A computer code, or program, that instructs a computer what to do.

style: A special look.

support: To hold up and help.

technology: Using science, engineering, and other industries to invent useful tools or to solve problems. Also a machine, piece of equipment, or method created by technology

version: A form of something that is different from others.

visual: Something that can be seen.

FOR MORE INFORMATION

BOOKS

Clay, Kathryn. *The Ultimate Guide to Drawing Adorable Animals!* North Mankato, MN: Capstone Press, 2026.

Longstreth, Sarah. *Learn to Draw ... Monsters!* New York, NY: Peter Pauper Press Inc., Rye Brook, 2023.

WEBSITES

Art for Kids Hub
artforkidshub.com
Check out some drawing classes on this website.

2024 Best Graphic Novels for Children Reading List
www.ala.org/gncrt/2024-best-graphic-novels-children-reading-list#top-ten
Check out the art in your next favorite graphic novel on this list of the American Library Association's best of 2024.

Publisher's note to educators and parents: Our editors have carefully reviewed these websites to ensure that they are suitable for students. Many websites change frequently, however, and we cannot guarantee that a site's future contents will continue to meet our high standards of quality and educational value. Be advised that students should be closely supervised whenever they access the internet.

INDEX